Warrior Women in American History

THE ROLE OF FEMALE DOCTORS AND NURSES IN THE CIVIL WAR

I0884168

Warrior Women in American History

THE ROLE OF FEMALE DOCTORS AND NURSES IN THE CIVIL WAR

Hallie Murray

Cavendish Square
New York

Published in 2020 by Cavendish Square Publishing, LLC

243 5th Avenue, Suite 136, New York, NY 10016

First Edition

Website: cavendishsq.com

Cataloging-in-Publication Data
Names: Murray, Hallie.
Title: The role of female Doctors and Nurses in the Civil War / Hallie Murray.
Description: New York : Cavendish Square Publishing, 2020. | Series: Warrior women in American history | Includes glossary and index.
Identifiers: ISBN 9781502655431 (pbk.) | ISBN 9781502655448 (library bound) | ISBN 9781502655455 (ebook)
Subjects: LCSH: Women physicians–United States–Biography–Juvenile literature. | Nurses–United States–Biography–Juvenile literature. | Military nursing–United States–History–Juvenile literature. |
United States–History–Civil War, 1861-1865–Medical care–Juvenile literature. | United States–History–Civil War, 1861-1865–Women–Juvenile literature.
Classification: LCC E621.M87 2020 | DDC 973.7'75 B–dc23

Printed in the United States of America

Portions of this book originally appeared in *Women Doctors and Nurses of the Civil War* by Lesli J. Favor, PhD.

Photo Credits: Cover, p. 3 akg-images/Archie Miles/Newscom; pp. 7, 18, 20, 49, 53, 55, 66-67, 69 Library of Congress Prints and Photographs Division; pp. 8-9, 10-11, 38, 42, 80 Bettmann/Getty Images; pp. 16-17 Stock Montage/Archive Photos/Getty Images; pp. 24-25 Smith Collection/Gado/Archive Photos/Getty Images; p. 28 Jason O. Watson/historical-markers.org/Alamy Stock Photo; p. 30 Maurice Savage/Alamy Stock Photo; p. 34 Museum of the City of New York/Archive Photos/Getty Images; p. 36 Charles H. Phillips/The LIFE Picture Collection/Getty Images; pp. 46-47 Corbis Historical/Getty Images; p. 57 ullstein bild/Getty Images; p. 61 Library of Congress/Corbis Historical/Getty Images; pp. 64-65 Kean Collection/Archive Photos/Getty Images; p. 72 Fotosearch/Archive Photos/Getty Images; p. 75 Netterville Briggs/Hulton Archive/Getty Images; p. 77 Mark Summerfield/Alamy Stock Photo; pp. 82-83 Cincinnati Museum Center/Hulton Fine Art Collection/Getty Images; pp. 86-87 Album/Alamy Stock Photo.

Contents

Introduction

The American Civil War officially began on April 12, 1861, when Confederate troops attacked the military base at Fort Sumter, South Carolina. But the ideological divide that caused the conflict had taken root much earlier. Residents of the states in the northern half of the country were increasingly morally opposed to slavery, and many had banned slavery on a state level. They didn't want slavery to exist in new territories either, hoping that the institution would eventually die out as more and more states outlawed it. The southern states, however, largely supported slavery because they depended economically on agricultural enterprises that were fueled by slave labor. As the North became increasingly powerful politically, Southern leaders worried that the federal government would soon outlaw slavery, sending many Southerners, especially wealthy slave owners, into financial ruin.

Southerners were particularly worried about Abraham Lincoln, so much so that the leaders of some states threatened to leave the Union if he became president. When Lincoln was elected in November 1860, that's just what they did: one by one, eleven Southern states seceded from the Union, forming the Confederate States of America. They were, in order of secession, South Carolina, Mississippi, Florida, Alabama, Georgia, Louisiana,

Born in 1809, Abraham Lincoln became the sixteenth president of the United States in 1861. He was elected for a second term in 1864 but was assassinated soon after, on April 14, 1865, by John Wilkes Booth.

Texas, Virginia, Arkansas, North Carolina, and Tennessee. Lincoln and other Republicans in the government declared that secession was illegal, and none of America's trading partners around the world recognized the Confederacy as its own country. Desperate to become a separate nation, the states of the Confederacy attacked the Union at Fort Sumter, launching the Civil War.

The Civil War was the bloodiest conflict in America's history. Men who had been friends, or even family, before the start of the war found themselves fighting against one another. The death toll was astronomical: at the Battle of Gettysburg, 43,000 people are said to have died, more than in any other battle in American history. At the Battle of Antietam, 22,720 men were recorded as dead, wounded, or missing, the

The Battle of Gettysburg is considered by many to have been the most important battle in the Civil War. This painting shows Pickett's Charge, a failed infantry push against the Union.

highest loss of life ever recorded on a single day in the history of the United States.

Some citizens in the Confederacy initially believed the war would be won quickly, but they soon realized how wrong they were. Both sides faced a rapidly increasing need for doctors and nurses to care for injured soldiers, as well as the infrastructure to deploy such medical professionals and new or makeshift hospitals to house the wounded. At the time, however, there were few nurses available, and certainly not enough doctors to meet the needs of the conflict. Nursing was not an organized profession, and no training courses for nurses were in place. Medical colleges had only recently begun admitting women. By 1861, just a few women had graduated

A United States Sanitary Commission (USSC) field hospital is shown here. The USSC was a relief agency created in 1861 by the federal government to bring aid to wounded Union soldiers. Many of its volunteers were women, who acted as nurses.

as doctors, and despite the desperate need for help on the ground, most of these women found it impossible to convince military authorities to commission them.

Furthermore, nursing wounded soldiers was considered quite unladylike. Although women had for years provided medical care to family and neighbors, many believed women of a certain class were too delicate to handle all of the blood and gore of an army hospital. Others thought it simply wasn't respectable for a woman, particularly a young, single woman, to enter a situation with so many men in the various states of undress required for treating wounds. In order to lessen this second fear, in fact, the superintendent of the Union army nurses, Dorothea Dix, required that all women in her employ be over the age of thirty and dress plainly.

Happily for the soldiers, countless women refused to bend to public opinion and jumped into nursing the wounded anyway. Those who couldn't find official work supporting the war efforts on either side volunteered, providing medical aid and other care across the nation in army hospitals, field hospitals, and makeshift facilities. In the North, more than three thousand women worked as paid army nurses, and two thousand others worked as volunteers or as affiliates of the US Sanitary Commission. In the South, thousands more women volunteered as nurses, although the Confederacy did not have an organized system of training or placing them. Women nursed the wounded on the battlefield, ran newly established hospitals, and took charge of medical assistance, cooking, and organizing care in camps across the country.

The flood of women nurses marked one of the first times in American history that so many women had dedicated themselves to work outside the domestic sphere. As a result, women on both sides of the conflict emerged with a newfound awareness of their capability to work outside the home. Through the efforts of women like British nurse Florence Nightingale, who founded the first secular nursing school in the world and advocated for allowing more women into the workforce, and Clara Barton, Civil War hero and founder of the American Red Cross, who inspired countless women to seek professional medical training, nursing and other female-driven professions began to gain acceptance. The Civil War, then, is more than a narrative of the struggle over slavery. It is also a narrative of an awakening of women to the field of medicine and the larger world.

1

The "Dragon" of the North

Though her sharp personality and no-nonsense attitude sometimes angered those around her, Dorothea Dix's authoritative approach was essential to her goal of protecting and caring for those who could not protect themselves. Dix is best remembered for her role as superintendent of female nurses in the Union army during the Civil War, but she also effected great change before and after the war as an advocate for social reform. She devoted her life to securing better care for those who were mentally ill or disabled.

As superintendent of army nurses, Dix's iron will and brusque demeanor made her a somewhat controversial figure. She had little patience for men who were threatened by her authority. On one occasion, she began a routine inspection without introducing herself to the doctor in charge. When he finally demanded to know who she was and why she dared to tell him what to do in his own hospital, she replied matter-of-factly, "I am Dorothea L. Dix, Superintendent of Nurses, in the employ of the United States."[1] The doctor's command over the hospital meant little compared to Dix's duties to the US government and the Union army. She was a force to be reckoned with, demanding the best of herself and others—not just those she supervised but all medical personnel she encountered.

Early Life and Activism

Born on April 4, 1802, in Hampden, Massachusetts (present-day Maine), Dorothea Lynde Dix was the oldest of three children. She lived the first dozen years of her life in New England, mostly in the thickly wooded terrain of northern Massachusetts. Her father, Joseph, tried his hand first at farming and then at preaching. Her mother, Mary, was a semi-invalid who spent much of her time depressed. At age six, Dorothea cared for her brothers, four-year-old Joseph and newborn John Wesley. When her father brought home piles of printed religious tracts to be folded and sewn together by hand, she was required to do this chore as well.

At age twelve, having grown to despise what seemed to her a grueling and loveless life, Dorothea showed up on her grandmother's doorstep in Boston. Two years later, having clashed wills with her grandmother, she went to live with her grandmother's sister, Sarah. She was much happier there. Soon, the fourteen-year-old Dorothea became a teacher in a girls' school. Still, the harshness of her life, the inability of her mother to care for her, and the stern rigidity of her grandmother all left a lasting impression on Dix's character. She said once, "I never knew childhood."[2] As an adult, Dix often appeared to others as stern, cold, and sometimes fearsome.

Dix did not discover the true passion of her life until, in 1841, she observed the treatment of mentally unstable people. Chained in small cells, they slept on the musty straw-covered floor, which also served as table and toilet. From this time until the outbreak of the Civil War, Dix devoted herself wholeheartedly to educating prison officials, lawmakers, and the public about the needs and rights of the mentally ill. Over the next forty years, she traveled throughout the United States and Canada, inspecting insane asylums and prisons and filing reports with legislators. In fifteen states and in Canada, her reports prompted the establishment of government hospitals for the mentally ill.

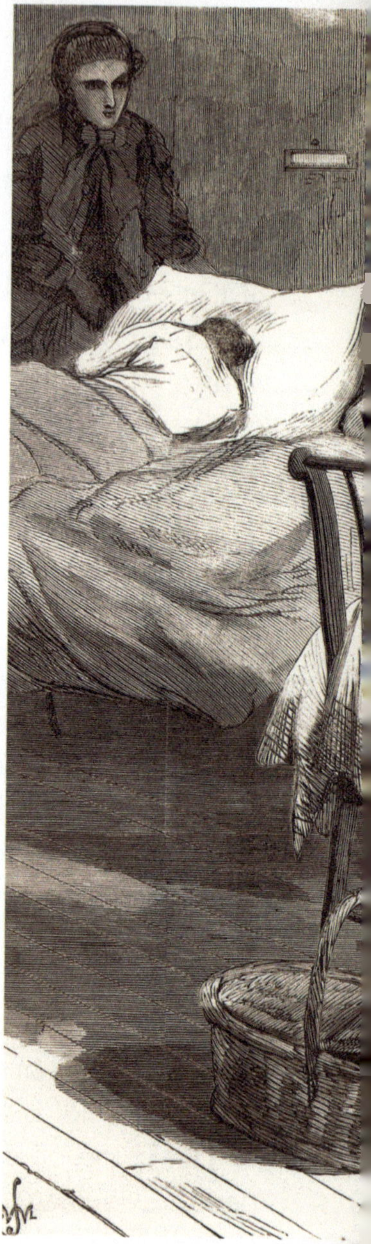

The Civil War Begins

In 1861, at age fifty-nine, Dix had accomplished remarkable reforms in the care of the mentally ill. But when the Civil War broke out, she identified a new area needing her service—the care of sick and wounded Union soldiers. She volunteered to head up the female nursing corps of the Union army, and on June 10, 1861, Secretary of War Edwin Stanton appointed her superintendent of female nurses for the Union army.

Dix approached her new role with the same vigor she had demonstrated in her previous campaigns. She had encountered resistance to her earlier reform efforts, and she encountered resistance again in her efforts to place women nurses in military hospitals. To many, the idea of a woman nurse seeing soldiers in various stages of undress was shocking. Just

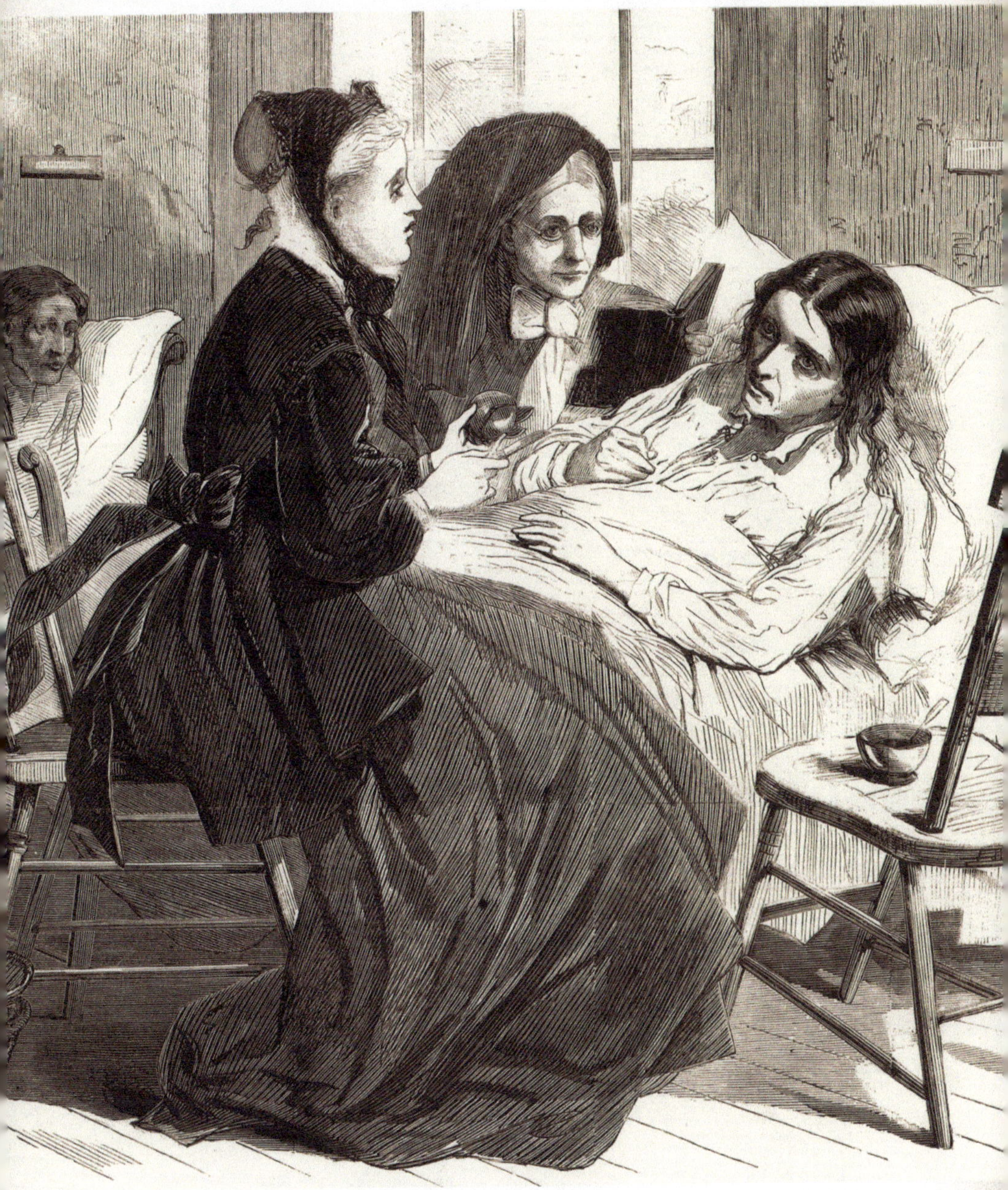

Two women comfort a patient of Blackwell's Island Asylum. The first mental institution in New York City, Blackwell's Island Asylum was established in 1834 and opened its doors to patients in 1839.

Dorothea Lynde Dix is best known for her activism on behalf of mentally ill people living in poverty and for acting as superintendent of army nurses during the Civil War.

as alarming was the thought that "gentlewomen" would nurse soldiers from all walks of life—ruffians as well as gentlemen—and that some men might use the situation to make improper advances. Adding to this fear was the fact that it was necessary for nurses to tend to soldiers confined in beds—the most improper setting imaginable by many. As if these objections weren't enough, Dix worried, with good reason, that society would question the morals of young, attractive, unmarried women who volunteered to nurse.

In her new job, Superintendent Dix interviewed female applicants, ensured they received training, and assigned them to military hospitals. She devised her own set of criteria for evaluating, hiring, and supervising the women nurses. In her typical no-nonsense fashion, Dix stated that

The United States Sanitary Commission

The United States Sanitary Commission was created in July 1861 to help meet the needs of the Union army, from transporting supplies to soldiers to providing medical care where needed. Since women couldn't serve as soldiers, many channeled their patriotism into volunteering with the Sanitary Commission, collecting donations, making uniforms, and working in hospitals as nurses. Dorothea Dix was appointed as superintendent of the Sanitary Commission by Edwin Stanton, the US secretary of war, and she convinced Union leaders that women should be allowed to provide medical and other care to wounded soldiers. Thanks in large part to Dix's efforts, the surgeon general declared in 1862 that at least one-third of army nurses should be female.

Union nurse Helen Louise Gilson wears a modest dress that Dorothea Dix might have approved of, though Dix may have disapproved of the dress's light color and decoration.

only women who were at least thirty years old and plain-looking need apply, with the idea that such women would be less subject to scrutiny while tending to soldiers than young, pretty women might be. Moreover, while at work the nurses had to dress in plain brown or black dresses with no frills such as ribbons, hoop skirts, or jewelry. Early on, she earned the nickname "Dragon Dix" as a result of these strict requirements and guidelines.

Women whom Dix hired received $12 per month. While the paycheck was welcome, especially considering the great number of volunteers who received no pay at all, it was much lower than that of the (male) surgeons, who received the large paychecks of up to $150.

At first, the Sanitary Commission's plan for the nurses was that they would staff the hospitals near Washington, DC, away from the actual fighting. Here, nurses washed wounds, changed bandages, administered medications, washed patients' faces and hands, and served meals. Before long, however, the need for nurses in field hospitals ballooned. In response, women nurses began traveling to field hospitals to tend the sick and wounded there.

Controversy and Criticisms

Dix was sometimes criticized for her inflexible approach to military nursing, and historians have described her as sour-minded. For instance, she was intolerant of volunteer nurses working at hospitals if they had not obtained their positions through the US Sanitary Commission. When she found civilian nurses in an army hospital, she attempted to get them sent home, regardless of the hospital's need for their services.

Despite criticisms of her personality and some of her decisions, Dix blazed ahead. She did what she was charged to do, including organizing and administering a network of medical care for Union soldiers. "Dix's job would have been difficult even for someone with a more agreeable personality," writes Ina Chang in *A Separate Battle: Women and the Civil War.* "She was responsible for screening thousands of nursing applicants, and she had to work with officials and surgeons who resented her authority. Even though her requirements for joining the nursing corps were rigid and she may have rejected very able women simply because they looked too stylish, she succeeded in sending out a clear message: Nursing was serious work."[3]

From her appointment in 1861 through the end of the war, Dix served as superintendent, working without pay at her own request. After the war, she returned to her humanitarian work for the mentally ill. She continued to campaign for better treatment of the mentally ill until her death in 1887, at the age of eighty-five. Though Dix may have been disliked by some for her sharp personality, it is her dedication to helping others and her ceaseless efforts on behalf of people who could not advocate for themselves that we remember most today.

2

"Entry Into Man's Domain"

When the Civil War first began, leaders in the Confederacy expected it to end rather quickly given the South's advantages in geography and personnel, so very little effort was put into creating military and medical infrastructure to support the war effort. As the conflict wore on, however, it became clear that the Confederacy needed to figure out a way to provide more official care to soldiers than just sending them to recover at civilians' homes. Established in 1862 at a preexisting barracks in Richmond, Virginia, Chimborazo Hospital was one of the first medical facilities constructed by the Confederate government to treat wounded soldiers. Dr. James B. McCaw was appointed to be surgeon-in-chief. The job of matron, or head of nurses, was offered to a young widow names Phoebe Yates Pember, who served in that position until the Confederacy's surrender at the end of the War.

Life Leading Up to the War

Phoebe Yates Pember was born on August 18, 1823, the fourth of seven children born to Jacob Clavius Levy and Fanny Yates Levy. A well-to-do Jewish family, the Levys resided in Charleston, South Carolina. Phoebe's father was known for his literary interests, and according to one of his great-granddaughters, he was "a gentleman of leisure."[1] Levy married Thomas Pember, a Boston gentleman, some time before 1860, but soon after the outbreak of the war, he died of tuberculosis. Pember returned to her parents'

home, and by the following year, they were living in Marietta, Georgia.

In Marietta, Pember became acquainted with Mrs. George W. Randolph, wife of the Confederate secretary of war. In November 1862, Mrs. Randolph asked Pember to serve as matron in Chimborazo Hospital. Pember later

Founded in 1670, Charleston (shown here in 1851) is the largest city in South Carolina. During the Civil War, it was a central city for secessionists.

described the idea as "rather a startling proposition to a woman used to all the comforts of luxurious life."[2] She worried that "such a life would be injurious to the delicacy and refinement of a lady [and] that her nature would become deteriorated and her sensibilities blunted."[3] Despite her misgivings, she took the post and reported for duty on December 18, 1862. Her pay "was almost nominal from the depreciated nature of the currency," and matrons such as herself "had no official recognition, ranking even below the stewards from a military point of view."[4]

Located at the western edge of Richmond, Virginia, Chimborazo Hospital had been taking in wounded Confederate soldiers for nearly a year by the time Pember arrived in late 1862. As the Civil War continued, the hospital expanded, eventually comprising 150 wards. At the time, it was said to be the largest military medical facility in the world. During the course of the war, some 76,000 patients passed through its wards. For the most part, each ward was a separate one-story building measuring about 30 by 100 feet (9 by 30 meters), holding forty to sixty patients. The wards were organized into five groups, with each group called a hospital and headed by a surgeon. Pember was matron of Hospital Number 2.

A Woman in a Medical Man's World

At Chimborazo, Pember was the first woman to report for duty as matron. Later, when she wrote about those first days, she titled a chapter "Entry Into Man's Domain."[5] Despite the need for personnel, Pember was not welcomed by most male physicians. Medicine was considered the domain of men, and Pember seemed an intruder. When she arrived for duty, she noticed that "there was no mistaking the stage-whisper which reached my ears from the open door of the office that morning, as the little contract surgeon passed out and informed a friend he met, in a tone of ill-concealed disgust, that 'one of them had come.'"[6]

One of the first battles Pember faced was over whiskey. According to Confederate law, matrons were to be in charge of dispensing "spirits," or liquor, to patients. (During the war, doctors commonly prescribed whiskey and other liquors, such as brandy, to the sick and wounded. A typical dose of liquor was 2 to 4 ounces.) When Pember sent a requisition for one barrel of whiskey (a one-month supply for her division), the surgeon in charge refused to release it. Pember recalled:

> The monthly barrel of whiskey which I was entitled to draw still remained at the dispensary under the guardianship of the apothecary and his clerks, and quarts and pints were issued through any order coming from surgeons or their substitutes, so that the contents were apt to be gone long before I was entitled to draw more, and my sick would suffer for want of the stimulant.[7]

But Pember refused to back down. On her side she had the Confederate law requiring liquors and other luxuries, such as coffee, tea, and milk, to be held and dispensed by the matrons. In her words, "The printed law being at hand for reference, I nailed my colors to the mast, and that evening all the liquor was in my pantry and the key in my pocket."[8]

Through her tenure as matron, Pember faced difficulties of one sort or another involving the whiskey. She was not free of the "onerous" responsibility until federal troops

This sign, erected by the United Daughters of the Confederacy in Richmond, Virginia, in 1953, marks Chimborazo Hospital, which at the time was the largest military hospital ever constructed.

Dealing with Rats

One of the many problems that Pember faced as hospital matron was soldiers who feigned injury or illness to avoid returning to active duty. They were dubbed "hospital rats" since they were as difficult to get rid of as the four-legged rodents. To many of these hangers-on, the hospital's store of whiskey had great appeal. Once, a hospital rat named Wilson attempted to force Pember to give him and his friends liquor. After grabbing her by the shoulder and speaking roughly, he received quite a shock when she reached into her pocket and cocked a pistol she kept there. She wasn't troubled by such demands again, at least not for a while.

took over the hospital at war's end. "There were many suspicious circumstances connected with this institution," she recalled. "Indeed, if it is necessary to have a hero for this matter-of-fact narrative, the whisky barrel will have to step forward and make his bow."[9]

The Importance of Non-Medical Care

At Chimborazo, Pember proved herself an exemplary caregiver, tending the physical needs of her patients while acknowledging their fears, dreams, and hopes. She appreciated it when grateful patients wrote poems and slipped them under her office door. She noticed, too, the artistic efforts of those who carved images from wood, bone, or other material. She listened to others tell about the battles they had been in, and she even listened when patients shared recipes from home. She wrote down one

Like whiskey, quinine was a key substance in doctors' and nurses' medical kits. Quinine has been used to treat malaria for nearly four hundred years, and Civil War doctors used it to ward off disease.

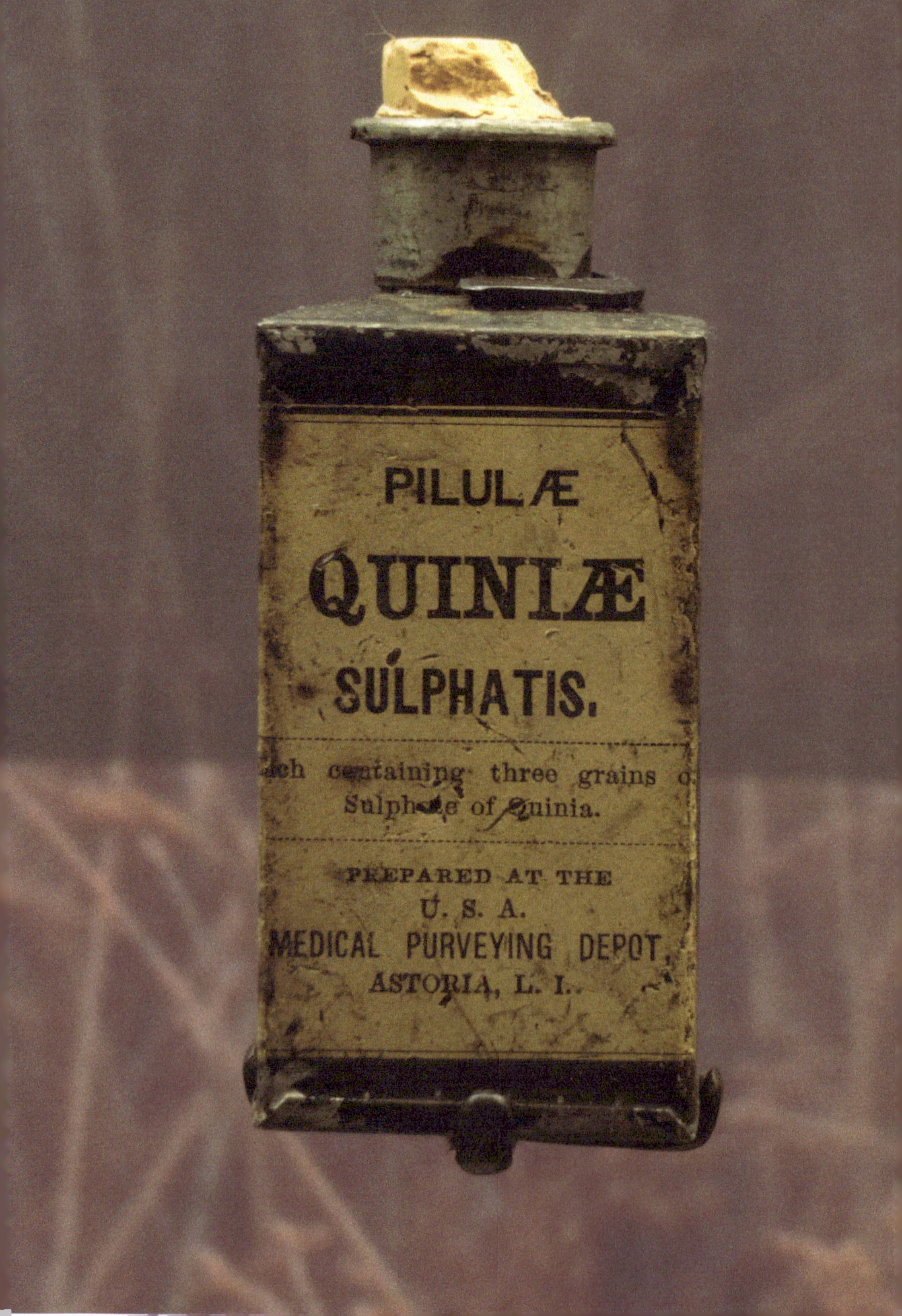

soldier's recipe for "sour soup," a concoction of buttermilk and egg-and-cornmeal dumplings, all flavored with "lots of pepper and salt."[10]

As the war wore on, Pember noticed a change in her patients' attitudes. Early in the war, they exhibited devotion to the Confederate cause, fighting what they believed to be an honorable war. She noted, "In no instance up to a certain period did I hear of any remark that savored of personal hatred. They fought for a cause."[11] But late in the war, they began to express a deep and personal hatred of the enemy. In part, the shift in view was inspired by the Union army's introduction of black troops, many of whom were former slaves. Even more so, Confederate soldiers' hatred was motivated by battles at Petersburg, an important rail center 23 miles (37 kilometers) south of Richmond, the Confederate capital. The series of battles that began there in June 1864 would culminate in the defeat of the South the following April.

After the Confederacy's surrender, Pember stayed at Chimborazo, overseeing the care of her patients during the transfer of authority from the South to the North. Finally, she returned to Georgia and published *A Southern Woman's Story* in 1879. She died on March 4, 1913, at the age of eighty-nine.

3

The Persistent Healer

Esther Hill Hawks and her husband, John Milton Hawks, were doctors and abolitionists who worked tirelessly to help provide medical care, education, and other assistance to former slaves and freemen in the South during the Civil War. At the start of the war, they lived in New England, where both had been born, and where Esther Hawks had earned her medical degree at the New England Female Medical College. But when Hawks and her husband saw the need for medical and other care for people of color in the South, they moved to South Carolina, and later to Florida, to provide assistance there.

Over 180,000 black men fought on behalf of the Union in the Civil War, but they often weren't treated as well as their white comrades-in-arms. Given that a central goal of the Confederacy was upholding the enslavement of black people, black soldiers who were wounded in the South faced particularly rough treatment.

In 1863, on the South Carolina Sea Islands, Hawks volunteered in the first army hospital for black soldiers and registered her displeasure at their conditions in her journal: the hospital was not "admited to the brotherhood of hospitals on quite an even footing," she wrote. "Favors were a little grudingly bestowed."[1]

One of the "annoyances," as she called them, was white soldiers getting bits of scrap iron at a blacksmith's shop and throwing them at her patients. Calling the black soldiers names was also a "frequent occurance."[2] Nevertheless, Hawks remained devoted to her patients, working as a physician and a schoolteacher to black soldiers on the Sea Islands and in Florida until the war's end.

Beginning a Medical Career

Esther Jane Hill was born on August 4, 1833, in Hookset, New Hampshire, to Parmenas and Jane Kimball Hill. An intelligent child with hazel eyes and black curly hair, she had four older and three younger siblings. After a public

The New England Female Medical College

Founded in 1848, the New England Female Medical College was the first school in the United States dedicated to training female doctors. Although there was a lot of sexism in the medical field, it was generally agreed that women were more suited to treating children and other women, particularly when it came to delivering babies. In 1874, the college merged with Boston University School of Medicine. Though only ninety-eight women ever graduated from the college with a full medical degree in its twenty-six years of existence, over three hundred women took classes there. Among these graduates were the first African American female physician, Dr. Rebecca Lee Crumpler, who graduated in 1854, and, of course, Esther Hawks.

Pictured here is the first woman to receive a medical degree in the United States, Dr. Elizabeth Blackwell. Blackwell was born in England and earned her medical degree in 1849 from Geneva Medical College.

school education, she decided she wanted to teach young people, but later she found a passion for medicine. In 1854, she married John Milton Hawks, a physician in Manchester, Massachusetts. She began studying Milton's medical books, absorbing the material so quickly that she was soon able to give public lectures on physiology. She then enrolled at the New England Female Medical College in Boston, studying anatomy, surgery, toxicology, and obstetrics. She graduated in 1857, a full-fledged doctor.

After the outbreak of war, Hawks went to Washington to obtain a post as an army doctor. To her dismay, the military refused to hire a female physician. Next, she applied to Dorothea Dix, superintendent of army nurses, for a position. Dix rejected her as well, possibly because Hawks did not meet Dix's minimum-age requirement. Not to be deterred, Hawks stayed in Washington until October, volunteering in the hospitals.

Union forces gained control of the Sea Islands off the coast of South Carolina, where they took over cotton plantations and claimed thousands of slaves (abandoned by their masters) as "contraband" of war. In April 1862, Hawks's husband took a job there as a physician, and Hawks followed him in October. She set to work as a teacher to former slaves, observing, "There has been no mental food for them any more than for the swine and cattle with whom their lives are shared ... They are all eager to go to school."[3] The following month, she extended her classes to include soldiers in the First South Carolina Volunteers, the first official black regiment in the Union army.

The First South Carolina Volunteer Infantry Regiment, shown here on dress parade, was a regiment of the Union army made up of escaped slaves from South Carolina and Florida.

Esther Takes the Wheel

Early in March 1863, the First South Carolina Regiment marched south to Jacksonville, Florida, leaving behind only the injured and sick. John Milton Hawks was placed in charge of a hospital set up especially for black soldiers. When injured soldiers were brought in from the Jacksonville expedition, he welcomed the assistance of his wife. Along with a nurse, Mrs. Strong, they bathed the patients and made up beds with clean sheets. Hawks noted with curiosity that many of the soldiers, who had never slept in clean sheets before, removed them, folded them carefully, and set them aside before sleeping on the bare mattress.

When John was sent to accompany "a secret expedition to the coast of Florida," Hawks took charge of the hospital. "Every morning at nine o'clock the disabled are marched down to the hospital in charge of a Sergent and I hold surgens call, for hospital and Regt. [regiment] and with great success."[4] Hawks was in charge of the hospital for three weeks, noting with pleasure that she performed the duties so well that headquarters did not notice it had neglected to appoint an officer to fill in for John.

On July 18, 1863, news came that 500 wounded men were en route to the hospital. The first group was brought in, 150 soldiers from the Fifty-Fourth Massachusetts Volunteer Infantry Regiment, a regiment of black soldiers commanded by Colonel Robert Gould Shaw. At the entrance to Charleston Harbor, they had attacked Fort Wagner, fighting valiantly but finally pulling back when they realized the white troops ordered to support them would not arrive in time. Hawks helped lay them on blankets on the floor, noting the men were "all mangled and ghastly."[5] Many former slaves from town came to their

Robert Gould Shaw was born in Boston in 1837. During the Civil War, he became the commander of the Fifty-Fourth Massachusetts Regiment, the first Northern all-black regiment of the Union army.

aid with broth, gruel (another name for porridge), fruits, vegetables, cakes, and lemonade. Hawks suspected that they went without food themselves in order to provide for the soldiers. Aid came, too, from the US Sanitary Commission. Hawks wrote, "No one, unless they have had the experience, can imagine the amount of work and worry needed in setting one of these vast military machines [hospitals] in motion!"[6]

Some of the soldiers developed gangrene, and the air inside the hospital stank so badly from decaying flesh that the afflicted men were moved outdoors. The stench combined with overwork and weakness from a recent fever finally caused Hawks to collapse. At first, she feared she would need to go home to Massachusetts to recuperate, but a week later she returned to work.

The Hawkses Move to Hilton Head

Leaving the Sea Islands in November 1863, Hawks accompanied her husband, now promoted to army surgeon, to Hilton Head, South Carolina. Here, as on the Sea Islands, she held classes for black soldiers and volunteered her medical services. A few months later, John was transferred to Jacksonville, Florida. Once again, Hawks set up a classroom for the soldiers, teaching when there was time to spare from her work in the hospitals.

Hawks was devoted to her work, but camp life was difficult. She missed having her own medical practice. "I often wonder," she wrote, "if I am doing just as much good as I might be in some other sphere—if I am wasting time which should be devoted to my profession."[7] Besides these doubts, other, more private pains intruded. She had been unable to conceive a child. "I have longed for this, prayed for it with all the passionate entreaty of a desolate nature. Why am I denied?"[8] Finally in August, she returned to Massachusetts for rest and recuperation.

Three months later, though, Hawks was back in Hilton Head, teaching school and assisting with medical work, duties she continued until the end of the war. That April, with the Union's victory over the Confederacy, Hawks was overjoyed: "The victory is complete, the surrender unconditional! The army disbanded; soldiers to return home, and all the offices paroled! The city is wild with rejoicing."[9] After the war, Hawks worked as a physician and a teacher, first in Volusia County, Florida, and then in Lynn, Massachusetts. She died at home in Lynn on May 6, 1906.

4

The Cyclone in Calico

A botanic physician from Ohio, Mary Ann Bickerdyke worked as a hospital administrator during the Civil War, a post she took up after hearing of the poor conditions wounded soldiers were subjected to. She was so beloved by her patients that she acquired the nickname "Mother Bickerdyke" for her nurturing attitude and the way she stood up for her patients. She had little tolerance for officers or physicians who tried to stop her from securing key supplies or caring for the wounded effectively, and she was so well respected that many incompetent leaders found themselves dismissed after run-ins with Bickerdyke. After the war, she became an advocate for veterans' rights and helped many secure pensions through legal assistance.

An Education in Botanics

Bickerdyke was born in Knox County, Ohio, on July 19, 1817. Her mother passed away when she was just seventeen months old, and she passed into the care of her maternal grandparents. After a few years, she was sent to live with other relatives. Thereafter, she moved from one relative's home to another, never finding a place

Mary Ann Bickerdyke, known as Mother Bickerdyke, was a determined and outspoken Civil War hospital administrator who would stop at nothing to make sure the soldiers in her care were treated well.

where she truly belonged. A journalist who interviewed Bickerdyke in 1861 reported that she grew up "a servant in the home of strangers."[1] It may be that because Bickerdyke had felt the lack of a mother's nurturing, she was able to sense what the soldiers, many of them young, needed in a caregiver.

Most sources say that Bickerdyke was one of the first women to attend Oberlin College, though it's difficult to verify this fact. She may have attended the Physio-Botanic Medical College in Cincinnati, but this, too, is up for debate. In an interview with a journalist in 1861, at which time the education in question would have been completed, Bickerdyke claimed only to have studied botanic medicine and to have taught herself practical nursing. Regardless of her formal education, or lack thereof, it's clear that Bickerdyke had experience in and knowledge of botanic medicine well before the Civil War began.

In 1847, she married Robert Bickerdyke, a widower with young children. Living in Cincinnati, the couple had three more children, though sadly the youngest, a girl named Martha, died when she was two years old. When Robert died in 1858 or 1859, Bickerdyke supported her family by practicing botanic medicine. Nature-based, this type of medicine relied on herbs, bark, roots, vegetables, water, and fresh air to treat patients rather than drugs such as opium or treatments such as bloodletting and purgatives.

A Whirlwind

In 1861, at the Galesburg Congregational Church, Bickerdyke listened as Reverend Edward Beecher read a letter from a doctor stationed with General Ulysses S. Grant's troops in Illinois. Describing soldiers suffering from typhoid fever and dysentery, the doctor pleaded for help. The congregation raised $500, and Bickerdyke volunteered to deliver the gift. Within a mile of the camp in Cairo, Illinois, she could smell a stench in the air. Once in camp, she saw piles of amputated limbs, dead dogs, and garbage.

After taking in the filthy, noxious situation, Bickerdyke rolled up her sleeves and went to work. She boiled uniforms and linens, all filthy and crusted with blood. She bathed the sick and wounded, wiping away battlefield grime and making sure each had clean clothes and fresh straw in his bed. With supplies she had brought, she cooked chicken dinners for everyone. Her whirlwind of activity inspired the nickname "the Cyclone in Calico."

The Cyclone in Calico kept going. After arranging for the care of her children back home, she turned her attention to the soldiers. She continued to treat patients at the military hospital in Cairo, often assisted by Mary Safford, a young woman who later became a physician. Although the doctor in charge of the hospital protested Bickerdyke's presence, General Grant ordered that she be allowed to stay, appointing her matron.

Mother and Commander

By 1862, Bickerdyke had joined the US Sanitary Commission. After doing a series of fund-raising speeches for Mary Livermore's branch of the commission, Bickerdyke received a thank-you gift of a magnificent labor-saving device, a washing machine, for her hospital. In a speech delivered in Milwaukee, Wisconsin, she asked her listeners,

"Suppose, gentlemen, you had got to give to-night one thousand dollars or your right leg, would it take long to decide which to surrender? ... I have got eighteen hundred boys in my hospital ... who have given one arm, and one leg, and some have given both."[2]

With her dedication to the care and comfort of common soldiers, not officers and surgeons, Bickerdyke truly embodied her nickname of "Mother." Dr. L. P. Brocket, described Bickerdyke in 1867: "She devoted her attention almost exclusively to the care of the private soldiers;

Authority from On High

While soldiers regarded Mother Bickerdyke with respect and affection, some of the surgeons and officers did not. Bickerdyke challenged their authority by doing things her way, whether or not they agreed. When Bickerdyke faced resistance from a doctor or officer, she declared, "My authority comes from God. Do you have anyone ranking higher than that?"[3] On one occasion, a surgeon, angry with Bickerdyke for accusing him of misconduct, complained to General Grant. Though Grant responded with humor, he meant every word he said: "Mother Bickerdyke outranks everybody, even [President] Lincoln. If you have run amuck of her I advise you to get out quickly before she has you under arrest."[4] On another occasion, when Bickerdyke caused a drunken surgeon to be dismissed, he went to General William T. Sherman to be reinstated. Sherman refused, saying, "I can do nothing for you. She [out]ranks me."[5]

This image shows five illustrations of women in the United States Sanitary Commission at work in hospitals, houses, and battlefields. In the center, a wreath surrounds the words "Our Heroines."

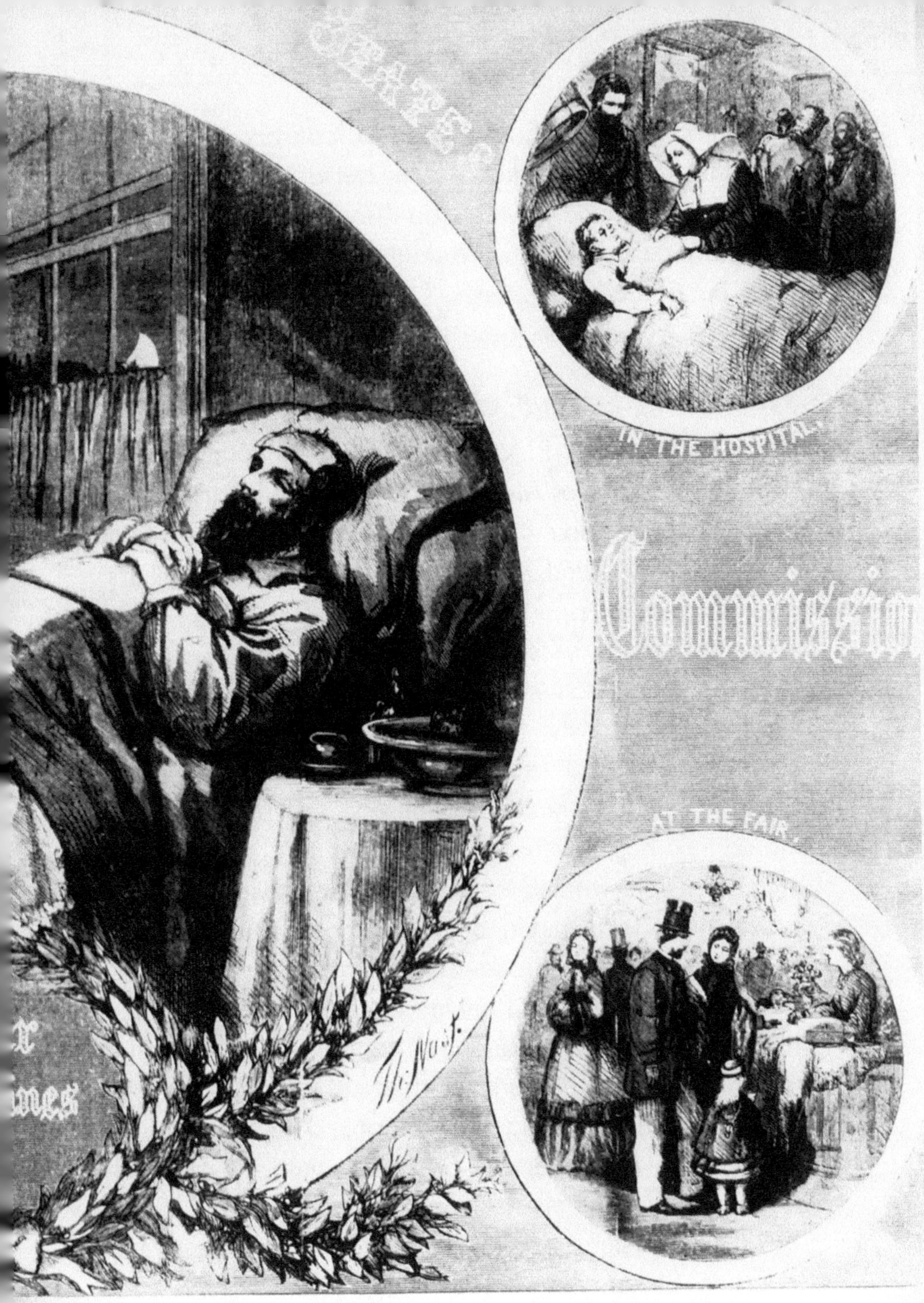
IN THE HOSPITAL.
AT THE FAIR.

the officers, she said, had enough to look after them; but it was the men, poor fellows, with but a private's pay, a private's fare, and a private's dangers, to whom she was particularly called. They were dear to somebody, and she would be a mother to them."[6] By all accounts, Mother Bickerdyke was dear to these soldiers.

Saving Lives through the End of the War

After Cairo, Mother Bickerdyke worked on the hospital transport ship *City of Memphis* on five trips as it carried wounded Union soldiers to Fort Donelson in northwestern Tennessee. She visited hospitals in Illinois and still others in Saint Louis, Missouri, and Louisville, Kentucky. There she joined efforts with nurses hired by Dorothea Dix, superintendent of women nurses for the Union army, as well as Catholic sisters who had volunteered. Then Bickerdyke moved on with Grant's troops down the Mississippi, setting up field hospitals as needed. In all, she set up about three hundred field hospitals, working with agents of the Sanitary Commission. She treated the wounded in nineteen battles.

One night following a battle, Colonel John A. Logan happened to notice a shrouded figure inspecting the lifeless bodies on the battlefield. Thinking the person might be one of those who robbed the dead, he sent an orderly to bring the intruder to him. The person turned out to be Bickerdyke, who had been searching for overlooked wounded. She declared, "Some soldiers in the frozen mud may be still alive. Do you expect me to sleep?"[7]

With earnestness and zeal and despite growing exhaustion, Bickerdyke worked through the end of the war. After the conflict, she received a continual flow of thanks from soldiers who claimed she had saved their lives. Until

John Alexander Logan was a Union general who served in the House of Representatives before and after the war and, later on, in the Senate.

her death on November 8, 1901, she occupied her time with one philanthropic cause after another, including the Chicago Home for the Friendless, a veterans' boarding house in Kansas, and the Salvation Army. She also worked for a time at the US Mint—a job she got with the help of her friend John A. Logan, now a US senator, who had watched her search for wounded on that dark battlefield.

The Angel of the Battlefield

Clara Barton is probably best known today as the founder and first president of the American Red Cross, which she established in 1881, but her work helping the wounded and ill began long before then. When the Civil War began, Barton was working in Washington, DC, at the US Patent Office, but she soon left her job there to help wounded soldiers in Baltimore, Maryland. She secured official permission from the War Department to transport supplies to regiments in need and worked directly on the battlefield, providing medical assistance and other care. Throughout the war, Barton worked to create the best conditions possible for Union soldiers to fight and heal, and her passion for providing aid to those in need persisted for the rest of her life.

A Childhood in Massachusetts

Born on Christmas Day, 1821, Clarissa Harlow Barton was the youngest of five children in a farming family in Oxford, Massachusetts. Her father, Stephen Barton, had been a soldier under General "Mad Anthony" Wayne in the Indian Wars. He often entertained young Clara with tales of his war days, acting out imaginary battles with her. She dreamed of becoming a soldier herself. Clara's mother, Sarah Stone Barton, was a hardworking, thrifty, outspoken woman. She signed antislavery petitions and, in Clara's words, "always did two days' work in one."[1]

To Clara, her siblings, who were ten to seventeen years older, seemed like four additional parents. "All took charge of me," she recalled, "all educated me, each according to [his or her own] personal taste."[2] From Stephen she learned math, and from David she learned "boy's" skills, including horseback riding, tying square knots, and throwing balls. Having learned to read by age three, she was attending school by age four. With Sally, who later became a teacher, she read literature and poetry. In this spirited family, Clara grew up shy, a personality trait she battled all her life.

At age eleven, when Clara got her first taste of nursing, she discovered the work to be fulfilling. When David fell from a barn roof and was badly injured, she cared for him and administered his medications. Later, when smallpox swept through the area, she nursed local victims.

At age seventeen, she began teaching school in a one-room schoolhouse and continued to teach for nearly fifteen years. But in 1853, after being passed over as principal of a school she herself had started, she left teaching, frustrated that women, no matter how qualified, were denied positions of authority.

Caring for the Wounded in Washington

At the outbreak of the Civil War, Barton was working as a copyist in the US Patent Office in Washington, the Union capital. She was thirty-nine years old, unmarried (not for lack of suitors, but by choice), and a staunch supporter of the Union. When she heard that soldiers in a Union regiment had been injured in Baltimore and would soon

Clara Barton is best known as the founder of the American Red Cross. During the Civil War, Barton worked as a nurse for the Union and was nicknamed "the Angel of the Battlefield" for her wartime efforts.

arrive by train in Washington, she rushed to the station. With a few other women, she wrapped their wounds with handkerchiefs.

Baltimore, she learned, was a city of mixed loyalties, with some citizens supporting the South and others supporting the North. The march of the Union regiment across the city to catch the train to Washington had attracted Confederate sympathizers, who taunted the troops and began flinging stones.

The soldiers fought back, shots were fired, and a riot ensued, ending in the deaths of four soldiers and twelve civilians. In response to the event, Barton wrote, "The darkest page in our country's history is now being written in lines of blood!"[3]

She learned that many of the soldiers had lost their baggage in Baltimore. They had the clothes on their backs, but nothing more. Right away, she went through the closets and pantries of her own house, gathering food and sewing supplies. Next she went to the merchants in town, persuading them to open on a Sunday so she could fill large wicker baskets with soap, food, and other items for the soldiers.

That spring and summer, Barton watched as thousands of troops poured into the city, setting up camp wherever there was space. Facilities such as the Treasury Department, the Navy Yard, and warehouses became makeshift campsites. One regiment set out bedrolls in the Patent Office where Barton worked. She went from place to place, nursing the sick and injured and delivering supplies. She placed an advertisement in the *Worcester Spy*, her hometown newspaper, inviting people to send bandages, salves, canned fruit, pickled vegetables, clothing, and

The Sanitary Commission wagons on the bottom left of this image carried medical and other supplies, like the ones Barton collected, to soldiers on the battlefield and in field hospitals.

other items for the soldiers. Within a few months, she filled her house and three warehouses with donations.

Out on the Battlefield

Talking to the soldiers, Barton learned of the horrifying conditions an injured or ill soldier faced at the battlefront. Supplies were limited, and many soldiers lay bleeding in agony on the ground, sometimes succumbing to infection, because there were too few doctors to treat all of the wounded. After learning of these conditions, Barton requested permission from the War Department to take supplies directly to the front lines. At first it was difficult to persuade authorities to allow a woman near the fighting. But finally she obtained a pass.

With her pass, Barton traveled from battle to battle with horse-drawn wagons loaded with medical supplies and food. She nursed soldiers by the dozen when they were carried away from battle. As she worked, shots sometimes split the air overhead. In some instances, the injured had to be hauled away quickly because as the battle moved closer, it overtook the grounds where wounded lay. In these instances, Barton stayed with her patients until the last possible moment. During these last-minute evacuations, her ability to ride a horse proved to be a life-saving skill.

On August 9, she heard about a battle at Cedar Mountain in Virginia. Stonewall Jackson had led 25,000 Confederate troops to victory over Union troops under John Pope. Three hundred fourteen Union soldiers had died in the battle, and 1,465 were wounded. More than 600 others were missing. When Barton arrived at Cedar Mountain four days later, she supplied surgeons with fresh dressings, provided soldiers with clean clothing, and

Henry Dunant was a Swiss businessman who founded the Red Cross after seeing the carnage of the aftermath of a battle in Italy. Barton followed in his footsteps after the Civil War.

prepared and served soup. All the while, shells burst in the background.

The End of the War and Beyond

From Cedar Mountain, Barton traveled by wagon to the Second Battle of Bull Run (known in the South as the Second Battle of Manassas). Wounded soldiers lay on hay that had been spread on the ground, and wagon upon wagon brought scores of additional injured. Soon they lay so close together that Barton feared treading upon an arm or leg as she moved among them. After dark, she feared that the accidental dropping of a candle would set the whole scene afire. She and other volunteers worked into the night, dressing wounds and distributing food and water. Beyond them, the battle raged on. As the enemy pushed closer, wagons began transporting the injured away. Barton refused to leave until the last of the wounded had been carried away. Thousands of Union soldiers died in the battle.

From the Second Battle of Bull Run, Barton traveled to a battlefield in Chantilly, Virginia. Then she headed to Antietam Creek, where, on September 17, the bloody Battle of Antietam was fought. As her brave service became known among Union soldiers, they began calling her the Angel of the Battlefield. Until the end of the war, she distributed supplies and worked as a battlefield nurse. Barton continually risked her life by nursing men at the front, saving countless lives.

After the war, she gave lectures on her wartime work, raising awareness for the vital service of trained medical personnel during war. She later traveled to Europe and worked for the International Red Cross. She was so

The International Red Cross

When Swiss businessman Henry Dunant witnessed the aftermath of a bloody battle in Italy during a trip, he was struck by the lack of medical attention available to the wounded. He worked with nearby towns to organize medical assistance for the soldiers. When he returned to Geneva, he decided to organize an institution that could help give that kind of aid wherever it was needed. In 1863, Dunant and fellow Swissman Gustave Moynier formed the International Committee of the Red Cross (ICRC). Barton became aware of the ICRC while traveling in Europe and was so inspired that she founded the American Red Cross on arriving home.

inspired by the organization that she began working to secure the support to create an American branch, and in 1881, Barton founded the American Red Cross. She served as president for twenty-three years before retiring in 1904, at the age of eighty-three. After a short retirement in Glen Echo, New York, Barton died on April 12, 1912.

6

The Doctor in Officer's Clothing

Dr. Mary Edwards Walker was a surgeon, women's rights activist, and abolitionist who worked as a volunteer physician during the Civil War, aiding wounded Union soldiers. Later on, she received her own appointment as assistant surgeon for the Army of the Cumberland. She was the first female surgeon to work for the army and the only woman physician to have received an official government appointment during the Civil War. As of 2019, Walker is also the only woman ever to have received the Congressional Medal of Honor, the highest U.S. military award. Signed by President Andrew Johnson, her citation declares that she "devoted herself with much patriotic zeal to the sick and wounded soldiers, both in the field and hospitals" and that she "also endured hardships as a prisoner of war four months in a Southern prison."[1]

The fifth of six children, Mary Edwards Walker was born on November 26, 1832, to Alvah and Vesta Walker. Along with her siblings, Mary grew up doing chores on the 33-acre (13-hectare) family farm in Oswego Town, New York. At a local school where her parents taught, she received her formal education. At home, her parents

Dr. Mary Edwards Walker was the only female surgeon appointed by the Union army. She received a Medal of Honor for her service in 1865, which can be seen here pinned to her lapel.

encouraged her to read widely, and she devoured her father's medical texts. She decided she would become a doctor.

At the age of twenty-one, Walker enrolled in Syracuse Medical College in New York. Her course of study included anatomy, obstetrics, surgery, and chemistry. In those days, a student earned a medical degree in two years, and Walker graduated in 1855, the only woman in her class. Soon after graduation she married Dr. Albert Miller, a former classmate. The marriage, however, was unsuccessful. After many years of separation, Walker obtained a divorce in 1869. She never remarried, nor did she have children.

The Start of the Civil War

When the Civil War started, Walker knew she wanted to serve the Union as a military doctor. She went to Washington and applied for a commission. While waiting for a response to her application, she volunteered in a makeshift hospital in the US Patent Office—the same office where Clara Barton worked. After learning that the army had denied her a commission, Walker stayed on as a volunteer. But true to form, she did not quit her quest to serve officially. She applied again, this time to the US surgeon general, Clement A. Finley. He also rejected her. It seemed no one with authority believed a woman could—or should—work as an army doctor.

For a time, Walker shifted her energies to the wounded pouring into Washington. She worked with confidence and authority. On one occasion, she went to a prison for deserters, concerned for their health, and she demanded entrance by saying, "I am Dr. Walker of the Union Army. I command you to let me pass."

Not long before, Secretary of War Edwin Stanton had appointed Dorothea Dix as superintendent of female nurses. On at least one occasion, Walker and Dix worked in the same hospital ward. Although Walker admired Dix's earlier work on behalf of the mentally ill, she had little patience for what she called Dix's "sham modesty" when it came to bedridden soldiers.[2] A patient's foot sticking out of the bedclothes was indecent enough to cause Dix to turn her head. In contrast, Walker matter-of-factly walked up and tucked the foot back in.

Seeking an Official Appointment

Hoping additional training would help get her a military commission, Walker attended the Hygeia Therapeutic

Dress Codes

Walker believed strongly in women's rights. Among the many causes she supported was dress reform. In the mid-1800s, women traditionally wore dresses with multiple petticoats and occasionally tightly laced corsets. Dress reformers resisted these fashions on the grounds that they were uncomfortable and impractical. They instead advocated for more sensible clothing choices. One of the most famous dress reformers was Amelia Bloomer, who preferred to wear a short dress or tunic over long, loose trousers with tight ankles, which came to be known as "bloomers." Walker herself experimented with all different skirt lengths. In 1870, as an adult, she was even arrested for wearing men's clothing.

College in New York City in 1862. Perhaps the most groundbreaking idea she studied there was that keeping patients' wounds clean could save lives. At this time, the dangers germs posed to wounds were poorly understood. Doctors did not sterilize operating tools, tables, or water used to clean wounds. Many patients who died could have survived if they had only been treated hygienically.

1
The Plain Dress.

Late in 1862, Walker returned to her volunteer work, this time in Warrenton, Virginia, where there was an outbreak of typhoid fever. Though she had not received an army commission, from this point forward she dressed in an officer's blue uniform of gold-striped pants, felt hat with gold braid, and a green surgeon's sash. In her quest for a commission, she wrote directly to President Lincoln. She described herself as a woman with "energy, enthusiasm, professional abilities and patriotism"[3] and said her strongest desire was to serve her country in a battlefield assignment. Lincoln's reply was speedy, but disappointing. He would not help her.

Over the next year, Walker traveled to Falmouth and then to Chattanooga at the front lines. Twelve miles (19 km) away, in Chickamauga, Georgia, 120,000 soldiers clashed at the bloody Battle of Chickamauga Creek. After two days (September 19–20, 1863), casualties were immense, with 16,000 Union soldiers and 18,000 Confederate soldiers dead, wounded, or missing. Tens of thousands of wounded Union soldiers poured into Chattanooga, where Walker had just

Many styles of women's clothing followed a similar formula of loose, ankle-length pants (known as bloomers) with a thigh- or knee-length tunic on top. Four popular styles of the past are shown here.

Both sides took prisoners of war during the conflict. The Confederate "rebel" prisoners shown here were held by the Union as prisoners of war at Camp Morton in Indianapolis, Indiana.

arrived. Eager to help, she worked at Gordon's Mill, southeast of Chattanooga. Here, Walker's energy and effectiveness impressed both Major General Alexander McCook and Major General George H. Thomas, the "Rock of Chickamauga." Both officers upheld their support of her when the medical director of the Army of the Cumberland, Dr. Perin, attempted to send Walker away. With McCook's and Thomas's support, she held her post.

Taken Prisoner by the Confederacy

During late 1863 and early 1864, besides doctoring soldiers at Gordon's Mill, Walker carried important medical supplies to the desperate civilians in the region. With Confederate troops in the area, Walker's forays behind enemy lines were risky, especially since she wore her army uniform. On April 10, 1864, she was captured by Confederate soldiers.

After a stop at a nearby Confederate camp where she treated soldiers, Walker was taken to a Richmond prison. Here, the trouser-clad woman doctor attracted curiosity and loathing. Captain Joseph Semmes reacted with venom. In a letter to his wife, he wrote that he and everyone else was "amused" and "disgusted" to see Walker in her Union uniform, and he called her "a thing that nothing but the debased and the depraved Yankee nation could produce—a female doctor." In a scathing conclusion, he declared, "I was in hopes that the General [Joseph E. Johnston] would have had her ... put in a lunatic asylum."[4]

Considering the horrid conditions of mental institutions of the day, Walker's prison may just as well have been an asylum. Rats skittered across the floor, insects crawled on her mattress, and the food was so poor that malnutrition caused a rapid decay in her eyesight.

Four months later, Walker was exchanged, along with other Union prisoners, for Confederate prisoners. To her surprise, the Union army then paid her $432.36 in salary for her service between March and August 1864. To Walker, who had before worked as a volunteer, the paycheck was an affirmation that she had found a legitimate place in the army. Her pleasure deepened when, a few weeks later, she was appointed acting assistant surgeon for the United States Army, with a salary of $100 a month. The position was that of a contract surgeon, so she was still a civilian, but the appointment confirmed her legitimacy to practice.

During the remaining eight months of the war, Walker's assignments took her first to a women's prison hospital in Louisville, Kentucky, and then to an orphanage in Clarksville, Tennessee, where she treated children and

After the Civil War, Walker became an activist and writer, particularly for the causes of health care and women's rights. She believed strongly that women should be free to wear whatever they wanted.

war refugees. Although her desire was to serve in field hospitals, she applied herself to her assignments.

The Congressional Medal of Honor

A few months after the war ended, Walker was awarded the Medal of Honor for her service during the war. Awarded for the first time, the Medal of Honor was for those who "most distinguish[ed] themselves by their gallantry in action, and other soldier-like qualities."[5] There was no doubt that Walker had demonstrated soldier-like qualities, but she had never fought in battle—the "action" named in the wording of the medal's purpose. Still, President Andrew Johnson, who signed her citation himself, supported Walker's candidacy.

Until the end of her life, Walker wore her Medal of Honor. Even after the medal was revoked, along with 910 others, in 1917, after a redefining of qualifications, she wore her medal defiantly. It was just as well, for sixty years later, in 1977, Secretary of the Army Clifford Alexander restored the honor to her posthumously. She is one of only eight civilians to have received the honor, which is now restricted exclusively to members of the military, and she is the only woman, as of 2019, to have received it.

The Female Captain of the Confederacy

The first woman to have been inducted into an army in America, not including those who had disguised themselves as men to receive appointments, was Confederate nurse Sally L. Tompkins. When legislation passed requiring all military hospitals have a military leader, Tompkins was commissioned as an army captain so that she could continue running her hospital in Richmond, Virginia. Tompkins is remembered as one of the most effective nurses of the Civil War, in large part because her private hospital had the highest survival rate of any army medical facility: of 1,333 patients under her care, only 73 died. This was an especially notable feat given that the Confederacy had far less formal infrastructure, medical or otherwise, than the Union did. Tompkins's strong will and significant financial strength allowed her to create real change, despite obstacles she faced for being a woman.

A Generous Inheritance

A native of Poplar Grove, Virginia, Sally Louisa Tompkins was born on November 9, 1833. A child of wealthy

Sally Tompkins, also known as the "Angel of the Confederacy," is best remembered as the woman who volunteered to run a Confederate army hospital out of the home of Judge John Robertson during the Civil War.

parents, her needs were generously provided for, even after her father's death. She and her mother moved to Richmond, where they lived on the inheritance left by Mr. Tompkins. After the US Civil War began in April 1861, twenty-seven-year-old Tompkins decided to use her inheritance to support the Confederate war effort. In Richmond, which soon became the Confederate capital, she opened Robertson Hospital to treat injured and ill Confederate soldiers.

Tompkins established Robertson Hospital after one of the war's early conflicts, the First Battle of Bull Run, fought on July 21, 1861. On this summer day, about thirty-seven thousand Union soldiers marched toward Richmond with an eye to take the city. On both sides, military leaders expected the war to end quickly, failing to anticipate how it would escalate. On that July day, civilian spectators accompanied the Union army, set up picnics, and sat back to watch the North trounce the South. But events played out differently than they expected.

The Union's advance toward Richmond was blocked by General P. G. T. Beauregard and his 22,000 Confederate soldiers. Joined later by 10,000 additional Confederates led by General Joseph E. Johnston, the Southern army routed the Northerners. Union soldiers and spectators alike retreated. Between 1,700 and 2,000 Confederate men were wounded or dead, and the injured poured into Richmond.

In Richmond, Tompkins leapt to meet the need for medical care. She saw that all available hospitals were overflowing, and soldiers were being nursed in private homes. A more organized and sanitary system of caring for the wounded would raise the injured soldiers' chances of survival. To this end, Tompkins appealed to a Richmond judge, John Robertson, for use of his large house. With his approval, she converted the house into a hospital, calling the facility Robertson Hospital. Besides herself and four slaves, volunteers helped care for its wounded.

Appointment to the Cavalry

Tompkins's heroic work did not escape the notice of powerful figures in the Confederate government, and her success at running an effective and self-funded facility probably saved her enterprise. Three months after she opened the hospital, Confederate president Jefferson Davis ordered all private hospitals for soldiers closed or placed under military control.

Too Bloody for a Lady

While female nurses cared for injured on both sides of the war, they were at first discouraged. It was more appropriate, people thought, if women stuck close to home, sewing and knitting clothing for the soldiers, collecting supplies, and providing similar "womanly" services. Though women had long been nursing family members and neighbors as a matter of course, traditional values hindered women from providing the same care to strangers, especially men. Even female doctors were thought to only be suited for caring for children and practicing midwifery. People believed that the bloody gore of wartime injuries, including amputations, head wounds, and the like, were too horrific for women to face. As the war progressed, however, the need for medical assistance quickly overwhelmed the male doctors and nurses available, and female volunteers rushed to help in hospitals and on battlefields.

Born in Kentucky in 1808, Jefferson Davis was a politician who represented Mississippi in the House of Representatives and the Senate and acted as secretary of war under President Franklin Pierce. He was the only president of the Confederacy, serving in that office for the duration of the Civil War.

Some of these medical facilities, which charged for their services, were providing inadequate care. Others were keeping in bed soldiers who army officials believed should already be back on duty. Tompkins was determined to keep her hospital under her own control.

She requested and was granted a meeting with President Davis, at which she asked that control of Robertson Hospital remain in her hands. Historians have speculated that President Davis agreed to her plan because she funded the hospital herself, while others point out the amazing survival rate that must already have been evident. At any rate, Davis devised an ingenious plan for allowing Robertson Hospital to remain under Tompkins's control. He commissioned Tompkins as a captain of cavalry in the Confederate army. As a result, she could keep her hospital open and operate it with the cooperation of the military. Of all the women who served the Confederate cause, Tompkins was the only one commissioned in the army.

Although located in Virginia, Robertson Hospital received wounded soldiers from across the South. This was no time for loyalties based on a particular state, but rather a time for all Southerners to unite. When Mary Boykin Chesnut, a volunteer, asked Tompkins whether there were any patients from the Carolinas in the hospital to visit and offer gifts to, Tompkins set her straight. All soldiers were to be treated with equal devotion. She told Chesnut, "I never ask where the sick and wounded come from."[1]

The Role of the Superintendent

As superintendent of the hospital, one of Tompkins's duties was to manage the preparation and distribution

After she passed away in 1916, Tompkins was buried with full military honors, befitting her station as a captain, in the Christ Church Kingston Parish Cemetery in Mathews, Virginia, in the grave under the monument shown here.

of food to patients. These duties fell to matrons, or head nurses, in army hospitals. For example, at the Union Hospital in Alexandria, Virginia, Jane Stuart Woolsey was superintendent of nurses and managed six different "special diets" for patients: the roast beef and pudding diet, the eggs and milk diet, the vegetable diet, the milk porridge diet, the beef tea diet, and the gruel diet. While monitoring the cooking, the matron made sure the correct items were included in each meal, including sweets as were allotted. As Woolsey wrote in *Hospital Days*, the superintendent of nurses "was expected to follow the food from the commissary storehouse down the sick man's throat."[2]

Over the course of the war, Tompkins remained a solid fixture at her hospital in Richmond, earning the respect of those around her. Writing in 1907 in *Belles, Beaux, and Brains of the [18]60s*, Thomas Cooper DeLeon described her as "original, old-fashioned and tireless in well-doing." He wrote that she was "as resolute as a veteran"[3] in her service to the Confederacy.

Affectionately known as Captain Sally, Tompkins operated her hospital for the duration of the war using her own money, supplemented with government rations. In June 1865, two months after the war ended, Tompkins closed the doors of Robertson Hospital. Upon her death on July 25, 1916, in Richmond, Virginia, she was buried with military honors.

8

The Scotland-Born Nurse

Kate Cumming is remembered as one of the most dedicated Civil War nurses because, unlike most other women in her position, Cumming remained a nurse through the end of the war. Her commitment to the job was a product of her enthusiastic support for the Confederate cause. Though her intense involvement in the war might suggest otherwise, Cumming actually wasn't born in the United States but in Edinburgh, Scotland, around the year 1830. Her family immigrated to America in 1835, when Cumming was still very young.

When the Civil War began, Cumming was inspired by Florence Nightingale's actions in Europe and Reverend Benjamin M. Miller's call for women to volunteer as nurses at the front, but her family wouldn't allow her to volunteer. At first, since her family disapproved, she only collected blankets and supplies for Confederate troops. But when she saw a regiment of soldiers leaving for war, many of them her childhood companions, she decided that she must volunteer as a nurse.

Heading to the Warfront

Along with about forty women, Cumming left her home in Mobile, Alabama, on April 7, 1862, traveling by train

Florence Nightingale was a British nurse who cared for soldiers during the Crimean War in the mid-1850s. Nightingale is widely considered the founder of modern nursing.

toward Corinth, Mississippi. Her father had given his support before she left, but her brothers-in-law asserted that "nursing soldiers was no work for a refined lady."[1]

The next day, they disembarked in Okolona, Mississippi, about 60 miles (100 km) from their destination, to wait for a permit to enter Corinth. It had rained heavily, the weather was dreary, and the women were dismayed to find that there were no available hotel rooms. Hearing of their plight, local families took the nurses in, and Cumming and a few others went to the home of Mrs. Haughton.

One of their hostess's granddaughters described the reception they were likely to receive from the doctors in the army hospitals. Cumming wrote in her journal, "It seems that the surgeons entertain great prejudice against admitting ladies into the hospital in the capacity of nurses. The surgeon in charge, Dr. Caldwell, has carried this so far that he will not even allow the ladies of the place to visit patients."[2]

On April 11, she arrived in Corinth, finally feeling as though she were "in the service in reality."[3] Cumming was nervous. Although she had never been near a large army or seen an injured man, she was about to see plenty of both. Upon arrival at the Tishomingo Hotel, which had been converted into a hospital, she was struck by its filth, gore, and tragedy. If she had harbored any romantic ideas about wartime nursing, those were dashed. "None of the glories of the war were presented here,"[4] she wrote.

The Horrors of War

The reality of the conflict was overwhelming. "Nothing that I had ever heard or read had given me the faintest idea of the horrors witnessed here," she wrote. "I do not

This 1895 painting by Thomas Corwin Lindsay of the Battle of Shiloh emphasizes how terrifying and bloody the Civil War was, with bodies and injured soldiers in the foreground.

think that words are in our vocabulary expressive enough to present to the mind the realities of that sad scene."[5] She saw wounded soldiers—Confederate and Union—lying "so close together that it was almost impossible to walk without stepping on them."[6] Her first tasks were to bathe patients and give them water to drink. She noted, "If I were to live a hundred years, I should never forget the poor sufferers' gratitude; for every little thing, done for them."[7] She was struck by the immensity of the suffering and the task ahead of her. "The foul air from this mass of human beings at first made me giddy and sick, but I soon got over it. We have to walk, and when we give the men any thing, kneel, in blood and water; but we think nothing of it at all."[8]

Cumming worked about two months at the Tishomingo Hotel before her group was transferred. On her last day there, she wrote, "We have seen many sad sights and much suffering since we came to this place; still, I shall ever look back on these two months with sincere gratification, and feel that I have lived for something."[9] In Okolona once again, she waited to see in which direction the army would move. In two months' time, the town had become swamped with wounded soldiers and refugees.

She spent her days nursing them in private homes, hospitals, tents, and at the railway station as cars full of wounded arrived. She sewed clothing for the soldiers, worrying about the quality of care they received. She wrote, "I hear many complaints about the bad treatment our men are receiving in the hospitals. I have been told that many a day they get only one meal, and that of badly-made soup, and as badly-made bread."[10]

The Traveling Nurse

After a ten-week visit to Mobile, Cumming traveled in earnest, working as a nurse in each city where she stopped. By the end of 1862, she had gone to Chattanooga, Tennessee, and Dalton, Georgia. From 1863 through the end of the war, she traveled throughout Georgia, Alabama, and Tennessee. At times, she helped move the wounded away from the advance of the enemy. On July 1, 1863, she wrote, "News has come that the enemy is across the river, and intends shelling the place. We are having hospital flags put up, but I do not see that they will do any good, as it is said the enemy pay no respect to them. We are packing up in a hurry to move. Our hospital

Unladylike Conduct

A subject that caused Cumming distress was the refusal of many women to nurse soldiers—or even to enter the hospitals—on the grounds that such actions were unladylike, even immodest. Many felt that a hospital was no place for a respectable woman, with all of the blood and wounded soldiers in various states of undress. Cumming noted, "Scarcely a day passes that I do not hear some derogatory remarks about the ladies who are working in the hospitals." She found it ironic that many sisters of the Catholic Church deemed it honorable to nurse soldiers, while other women who considered themselves Christian thought the same actions to be wrong. Cumming concluded that "in truth, none but the 'refined and modest' have any business in hospitals"[11]—implying that those who refused to help were the unladylike ones.

being near the river, we will be honored by the first shot."[12]

During her travels, she kept a journal. While early entries describe the newness of nursing and war and soldiers, her thoughts gradually turned to the political leaders' strategies, her hopes for the war's outcome, her worry for the soldiers, and her sorrow each time a patient died.

Despite the continual loss of lives, Cumming tried to remain upbeat and optimistic. Weeks before the war ended, she wrote:

> We seem to be completely hemmed in on all sides. I hear that the long-expected attack on Mobile has at last begun, and that a large force is moving against Selma and Montgomery. One

Catholic nuns volunteered as nurses on both sides of the Civil War. This woodcut, entitled "Our Women and the War" includes a Catholic sister nursing a man on the far left.

> of the largest armies yet massed by the North is investing Richmond; Sherman and his vandals are in the very heart of the country, and a large army coming in by Wilmington—which is now in their hands; Charleston is closely besieged. Not one ray of light gleams from any quarter. It seems like hoping against hope; but my strong faith in the justice of our cause makes failure to me an impossibility.[13]

A few weeks later, after learning that Confederate president Jefferson Davis was captured, she wrote, "The patriot is now a prisoner."[14] The war was over. Cumming returned to Mobile, where she was active in church, community activities, the United Daughters of the Confederacy, and the United Confederate Veterans. She never married. After her death on June 5, 1909, she was buried at Saint John's Episcopal Church in Mobile.

Chronology

1860 **December** South Carolina secedes from the United States.

1861 **January–February** Mississippi, Florida, Alabama, Georgia, Louisiana, and Texas also secede. With South Carolina, they form a provisional government, the Confederate States of America, with Jefferson Davis as president.

April 12 Confederate soldiers fire on Fort Sumter in Charleston, South Carolina.

April–May Four more states, Virginia, Arkansas, Tennessee, and North Carolina, join the Confederacy.

July The First Battle of Bull Run (Battle of Manassas) takes place.

August The Battle of Wilson's Creek occurs.

1862 **March** Battle between the ships *Monitor* and *Virginia* (also known as the *Merrimack*) occurs.

April The Battle of Shiloh takes place.

June–July The Seven Days' Battle takes place.

August The Second Battle of Bull Run (Second Battle of Manassas) occurs.

September The Battle of Antietam takes place.

October The Battle of Perryville occurs.

December The Battle of Fredericksburg occurs.

1863 **January 1** Lincoln issues the Emancipation Proclamation.

May The Battle of Chancellorsville takes place.

May–July The Siege of Vicksburg, Mississippi, occurs.

July The Battle of Gettysburg is fought.

November 19 Lincoln delivers the Gettysburg Address.

1864 **August** The Battle of Mobile Bay takes place.

September General Sherman captures Atlanta.

October The Battle of Cedar Creek is fought.

November Lincoln is reelected president.

November–December General Sherman's 300-mile (483 km) "March to the Sea" from Atlanta to the Atlantic Ocean destroys anything useful to the Confederates.

1865 **April 2** Union forces capture Richmond, Virginia, the Confederacy's capital.

April 9 General Lee surrenders to General Grant at Appomattox Court House in Virginia.

April 14 President Lincoln is assassinated.

April–May The remaining Confederate forces surrender.

December 18 The Thirteenth Amendment is ratified, abolishing slavery.

Chapter Notes

Chapter 1

The "Dragon" of the North

1. Elizabeth Schleichert, *The Life of Dorothea Dix* (Frederick, MD: Twenty-First Century Books, 1992), p. 70.
2. Schleichert, p. 13.
3. Ina Chang, *A Separate Battle: Women and the Civil War* (New York: Lodestar Books, 1991), p. 36.

Chapter 2

"Entry Into Man's Domain"

1. Phoebe Yates Pember, *A Southern Woman's Story: Life in Confederate Richmond*, Bell Irvin Wiley, editor (St. Simons Island, GA: Mockingbird Books, 1959), p. 2.
2. Pember, p. 16.
3. Pember, p. 16.
4. Pember, p. 15.
5. Pember, p. 15.
6. Pember, p. 17.
7. Pember, pp. 24–25.
8. Pember, p. 25.
9. Pember, pp. 53–54.
10. Pember, p. 8.
11. Pember, p. 62.

Chapter 3

The Persistent Healer

1. Esther Hill Hawks, *A Woman Doctor's Civil War*, Gerald Schwartz, editor (Columbia, SC: University of South Carolina Press, 1984), p. 49.
2. Hawks, p. 49.

3. Hawks, p. 38.
4. Hawks, p. 49.
5. Hawks, p. 50.
6. Hawks, p. 51.
7. Hawks., p. 71.
8. Hawks, p. 68.
9. Hawks, p. 129.

Chapter 4

The Cyclone in Calico

1. Beatrice Levin, *Women and Medicine*, 3rd ed. (Lanham, MD: Scarecrow Press, 2002), p. 84.
2. Sylvia G. Dannett, editor, *Noble Women of the North* (New York: Thomas Yoseloff, 1959), p. 232.
3. Levin, p. 85.
4. Mary Elizabeth Massey, *Bonnet Brigades: American Women and the Civil War* (New York: Alfred A. Knopf, 1966), p. 49.
5. L. P. Brocket and Mary C. Vaughan, *Women at War: A Record of Their Patriotic Contributions, Heroism, Toils and Sacrifice During the Civil War* (1867), reprinted (Stamford, CT: Longmeadow, 1993), p. 176.
6. Brocket and Vaughan, pp. 172–173.
7. Levin, p. 85.

Chapter 5

The Angel of the Battlefield

1. Cathy East Dubowski, *Clara Barton: Healing the Wounds* (Englewood Cliffs, NJ: Silver Burdett Press, 1991), p. 18.
2. Dubowski, p. 17.
3. Stephen B. Oates, *A Woman of Valor: Clara Barton and the Civil War* (New York: Free Press, 1994), p. 5.

Chapter 6

The Doctor in Officer's Clothing

1. Allen Mikaelian, *Medal of Honor: Profiles of America's Military Heroes from the Civil War to the Present* (New York: Hyperion, 2002), p. 1.
2. Mikaelian, p. 6.
3. Mikaelian, p. 7.
4. Karen Zeinert, *Those Courageous Woman of the Civil War* (Brookfield, CT: Millbrook Press, 1998), p. 49.
5. Mikaelian, p. xviii.

Chapter 7

The Female Captain of the Confederacy

1. Susan Provost Beller, *Confederate Ladies of Richmond* (Brookfield, CT: Twenty-First Century Books, 1999), p. 46.
2. Jane Stuart Woolsey, *Hospital Days: Reminiscence of a Civil War Nurse* (Roseville, MN: Edinborough Press, 1996), p. 21.
3. Thomas Cooper DeLeon, *Belles, Beaux, and Brains of the 60's* (New York: G. W. Dillingham Company, 1907), p. 389.

Chapter 8

The Scotland-Born Nurse

1. Kate Cumming, *Kate: The Journal of a Confederate Nurse,* Richard Barksdale Harwell, editor (Baton Rouge, LA: Louisiana State University Press, 1959), p. xii.
2. Cumming, p. 12.
3. Cumming, p. 13.
4. Cumming, p. 14.
5. Cumming, p. 14.
6. Cumming, p. 14.

7. Cumming, p. 15.
8. Cumming, p. 15.
9. Cumming, p. 40.
10. Cumming, p. 49.
11. Cumming, p. 179.
12. Cumming, p. 111.
13. Cumming, p. 266.
14. Cumming, p. 284.

Glossary

abolition A movement to abolish, or end, slavery.

amputate To surgically remove all or part of a limb.

Civil War The conflict from 1861 to 1865 between the Northern states (the Union) and the Southern states (the Confederacy), which had seceded from the Union.

Confederacy The eleven Southern states that seceded from the United States in 1860 and 1861; the South. Members of the Confederacy were called Confederates.

field hospital A temporary hospital set up near a field of battle.

freeman A person who is not enslaved. By the time of the Civil War, "freeman" was primarily used to refer specifically to a black person who was not a slave.

gangrene A condition where body tissue dies from lack of blood, sometimes because of infection. Tissue affected by gangrene usually needs to be cut off the body to preserve the living tissue around it.

invalid Someone who is ill or weakened by injury.

matron A head nurse.

opium An addictive narcotic drug that consists of the dried juice of the opium poppy and that was sometimes administered to relieve extreme pain.

regiment A unit of soldiers.

secede To withdraw from an organization; as a noun, secession.

spirit A strong liquor like whiskey or vodka. Spirits were used medicinally at the time of the Civil War.

Union Northern states loyal to the federal government headed by President Abraham Lincoln during the Civil War; the North. Members of the Union were called Federals.

United States Sanitary Commission The organization created by an order of President Abraham Lincoln to train nurses and improve sanitary conditions for the Union army.

typhoid fever A bacterial infection common in conditions where there is poor hygiene or sanitation that often proved fatal before the use of antibiotics.

veteran A former soldier.

Bibliography

Alcott, Louisa May. *Hospital Sketches*. Cambridge, MA: Belknap Press, 1960.

Baker, Nina Brown. *Cyclone in Calico: The Story of Mary Ann Bickerdyke*. Boston, MA: Little, Brown, 1952.

Beers, Fannie A. *Memories: A Record of Personal Experience and Adventure During Four Years of War*. Philadelphia: J. B. Lippincott, 1889.

Beller, Susan Provost. *Confederate Ladies of Richmond*. Brookfield, CT: Twenty-First Century Books, 1999.

Brocket, L. P., and Mary C. Vaughan. *Women at War: A Record of Their Patriotic Contributions, Heroism, Toils and Sacrifice During the Civil War*. Stamford, CT: Longmeadow, 1993.

Chang, Ina. *A Separate Battle: Women and the Civil War*. New York: Lodestar Books, 1991.

Cordell, M. R. *Courageous Women of the Civil War: Soldiers, Spies, Medics, and More*. Chicago: Chicago Review Press, 2016.

Cumming, Kate. *Kate: The Journal of a Confederate Nurse*. Richard Barksdale Harwell, ed. Baton Rouge, LA: Louisiana State University Press, 1959.

Dannett, Sylvia G., ed. *Noble Women of the North*. New York: Thomas Yoseloff, 1959.

Denney, Robert E. *Civil War Medicine: Care and Comfort of the Wounded*. New York: Sterling Publishing, 1994.

Devine, Shauna. *Learning from the Wounded: The Civil War and the Rise of American Medical Science.* Chapel Hill, NC: University of North Carolina Press, 2014.

Doherty, Kieran. *Congressional Medal of Honor Recipients.* Springfield, NJ: Enslow Publishers, 1998.

Dubowski, Cathy East. *Clara Barton: Healing the Wounds.* Englewood Cliffs, NJ: Silver Burdett Press, 1991.

Hawks, Esther Hill. *A Woman Doctor's Civil War.* Gerald Schwartz, ed. Columbia, SC: University of South Carolina Press, 1984.

Hillstrom, Kevin, and Laurie Collier Hillstrom. *American Civil War Almanac.* Lawrence W. Baker, ed. Detroit, MI: UXL Gale Group, 2000.

Hillstrom, Kevin, and Laurie Collier Hillstrom. *American Civil War Biographies.* 2 volumes. Lawrence W. Baker, ed. Detroit, MI: UXL Gale Group, 2000.

Kent, Jacqueline C. *Women in Medicine.* Minneapolis: Oliver Press, 1998.

Levin, Beatrice. *Women and Medicine.* 3rd ed. Lanham, MD: Scarecrow Press, 2002.

Livermore, Mary A. *My Story of the War.* New York: Arno Press, 1972.

Maher, Mary Denis. *To Bind Up the Wounds: Catholic Sister Nurses in the U.S. Civil War.* Baton Rouge, LA: Louisiana State University Press, 1989.

Marshall, Helen E. *Dorothea Dix: Forgotten Samaritan.* New York: Russell and Russell, 1967.

McCurry, Stephanie. *Women's War: Fighting and Surviving the American Civil War*. Boston, MA: Belknap Press, 2019.

Mikaelian, Allen. *Medal of Honor: Profiles of America's Military Heroes from the Civil War to the Present*. New York: Hyperion, 2002.

Oates, Stephen B. *A Woman of Valor: Clara Barton and the Civil War*. New York: Free Press, 1994.

Pember, Phoebe Yates. *A Southern Woman's Story: Life in Confederate Richmond*. Bell Irvin Wiley, ed. St. Simons Island, GA: Mockingbird Books, 1959.

Sanitary Commission of the United States Army: A Succinct Narrative of Its Works and Purposes. New York: Arno Press, 1972.

Schleichert, Elizabeth. *The Life of Dorothea Dix*. Frederick, MD: Twenty-first Century Books, 1992.

Sherrow, Victoria. *Women and the Military: An Encyclopedia*. Denver, CO: ABC-CLIO, 1996.

Wilbur, C. Keith. *Civil War Medicine 1861–1865*. Philadelphia: Chelsea House, 1995.

Further Reading

Books

Bradley, Michael. *Civil War Myths and Legends: The True Stories Behind History's Mysteries*. 2nd ed. Guilford, CT: Globe Pequot Press, 2019.

Cummings, Judy Dodge. *The Civil War: The Struggle that Divided America*. White River Junction, VT: Nomad Press, 2017.

Monson, Marianne. *Women of the Blue and Gray: True Stories of Mothers, Medics, Soldiers, and Spies of the Civil War.* Salt Lake City, UT: Shadow Mountain Publishing, 2018.

Seiple, Samantha. *Louisa on the Front Lines: Louisa May Alcott in the Civil War*. New York, NY: Seal Press, 2019.

Websites

American Battlefield Trust

www.battlefields.org

The American Battlefield Trust works to preserve battlefields around the country and has information and documents from a number of different battles and conflicts, including the Civil War.

American Civil War Museum
acwm.org
The American Civil War Museum has one of the largest and most thorough collections of Civil War artifacts and documents in the country, much of which can be viewed through its website.

American Red Cross
www.redcross.org
The American Red Cross is a national organization that is primarily staffed by volunteers of all ages. It helps provide aid and raise money for people in need across the United States.

National Women's History Museum
www.womenshistory.org
The website for the National Women's History Museum in Alexandria, Virginia, offers digitized exhibits, articles, and other resources about women throughout American history.

Index